William Morris Stewart

Analysis of the Functions of Money

William Morris Stewart

Analysis of the Functions of Money

ISBN/EAN: 9783337416256

Printed in Europe, USA, Canada, Australia, Japan

Cover: Foto ©Suzi / pixelio.de

More available books at **www.hansebooks.com**

ANALYSIS

OF THE

Functions of Money

BY

WM. M. STEWART

U. S. SENATOR FROM NEVADA.

WASHINGTON, D. C.:
WM. BALLANTYNE & SONS,
428 SEVENTH ST. N. W.,
1898.

DEDICATION.

This little volume is dedicated to the young men and women of the United States who are contemplating matrimony with its inevitable responsibilities. The comforts of life with which the young women of this country have been surrounded in the homes of their fathers, built in the better days of the Republic, cannot be provided by the young men of the present day on account of the hard conditions which environ them. The families and friends of young women oppose their marriage with young men otherwise worthy, on account of the fear that it will be impossible for the united efforts of both to save them from poverty and want.

The author believes that a careful study of this book will enable the people, through the intelligent exercise of the elective franchise, to restore the conditions enjoyed by former generations, when happy homes were established throughout our vast domain. If this can be accomplished, the barrier which fear of poverty has erected between the young men and women of the country will be removed and the sacrament of marriage will again promise happiness, prosperity and progress.

WM. M. STEWART.

WASHINGTON, D. C., April 12, 1898.

CONTENTS.

	PAGE.
MONEY	7
VALUE	19
PRICE	23
BIMETALLISM	31
RATIO	41
MOTIVE FOR DEMONETIZATION	51
MONEY IS NATIONAL	57
PARITY	69
FOREIGN COMMERCE	75
LABOR INTERESTS	81
BANK CURRENCY	85

MONEY.

Money is a fundamental condition of the existence of society. Men must live in society or perish. No human being was ever able to prolong his existence for any considerable time without the use of what others produce. All the authors on political economy agree that mere barter without money involves isolation and extermination, which the most primitive savages avert by the invention of some kind of money. If ever a tribe of savages existed without using sticks, shells or some kind of tokens as money, the fact has not been recorded and the possibility of such existence is denied.

As life is the potential principle or force by which the organs of animals and plants are started and continued in the performance of their several and co-operative functions, so money is the potential principle or force through the workings of which men associate their efforts and produce industrial society.

As law is "a rule or method of action or order of sequence," which has not been fully described in the thousands of law books published for that purpose, and can never be described in detail, so the infinite variety of uses to which money may be applied will never be written in books. Every attempt to define law by enumerating the various laws of nature and of man, and describing their functions, has been a total failure, and the attempts to define money by a full description of its uses have been equally unsuccessful.

Aristotle comprehended the money question and pointed out in a simple statement the difference between commodities produced by labor, and money created by law. In his "Ethics and Politics," 3rd London edition, 1813, vol. 1, page 375, he says:

"The comforts of life require an interchange "of different works and exertions. The brick-"layer, for example, must exchange the pro-"duction of his labor with the shoemaker; and "the bargain will be just when the works ex-"changed bear the same proportion to each "other as do the exertions of the artisans by "whom they were produced. If the exertions

"of the bricklayer be more valuable for their
"duration or their difficulty than those of the
"shoemaker, the works produced by the latter
"must, to render the bargain equal, bear the
"same proportion numerically to those pro-
"duced by the former; thus, if the bricklayer
"has consumed a thousand times as much labor
"in making a house as the shoemaker has done
"in making a pair of shoes, a thousand pairs of
"shoes must be given for one house. The same
"thing happens with respect to all other acts
"which derive their whole utility from the mu-
"tual exchange of different sorts of labor, and
"which could not long be maintained unless
"the exertions of one artisan in one way were
"nearly balanced and compensated by those
"of another artisan in another. A community
"could not subsist composed wholly of physi-
"cians or wholly of husbandmen; it must con-
"sist of physicians and husbandmen; and other
"classes of individuals employed in different
"trades and different professions. But that
"operations and works of such different kinds
"should be fairly exchanged for each other, it is
"necessary that they should be nearly commen-
"surate; that is, that all of them should be

"capable of being estimated with tolerable ac-
"curacy by comparison with one common
"measure. Hence the introduction of money;
"by means of which all those operations and
"works are compared in value with each other,
"and their relative excesses or deficiencies as-
"certained with sufficient correctness for all
"practical purposes. In reality, value depends
"on the mutual wants of men, which form the
"great bond of society; for unless their wants
"were mutual, exchange could not be effected;
"but money is used by convention as the repre-
"sentative of all things wanted; since it serves
"as a pledge and surety, that whenever those
"wants occur they will be speedily gratified;
"and its name is derived from the word signi-
"fying law, which indicates that it is founded,
"not on nature, but on convention; and that
"human laws, which have thought fit to em-
"ploy it as a measure of value, may, at pleas-
"ure, set this use of it aside, and employ some
"other measure in its stead. Money, which
"represents the value of all other things, va-
"ries in its own; but its variations are less
"considerable than those of most other sub-
"stances. It serves, therefore, to fix their

"price, and to render them commensurate with "each other, thus performing a function essen- "tial to the existence of civil society; for com- "munities could not subsist without exchange, "nor exchange without equality, nor equality "without a common measure. The various "kinds of labor, and the works thereby ef- "fected, cannot, indeed, be accurately com- "pared and exactly measured, either by each "other or even by money; but they may, by "means of the latter, be estimated with suffi- "cient correctness for maintaining that com- "mercial intercourse which is essential to the "supply of our numerous exigencies."

The great variety of things which have been used as money, at different times in different countries, has associated money with commodities and misled many of the so-called econo- mists. The number of men in high official station, and of professors of political economy in American colleges, who regard money as a commodity and not a function created by law, seems to be constantly increasing. The number and variety of commodities that were once used as money, and by law or cus- tom would pay debts and buy property.

which now possess no money function, ought
to suggest to political economists that such
commodities were never money in themselves,
but that the money function connected with
them, while it existed, was created and maintained by force of some law which the people
obeyed. The highest courts of England and
America agree with Aristotle, and hold that
money is the creation of law, and that every
sovereign power may create money without regard to the material which is used for that
purpose.

The leading case in England is known as
the Mixed Money case. It arose in the reign
of Elizabeth, and is reported in Davis' Reports
of Decisions of that period, page 48. It was
decided in that case that the power to create
money, make it a full legal-tender, and to use
any material whatever suitable for that purpose was inherent in every independent state,
and that the money current by law at the date
of payment was the money of the contract, because all contracts were made with a view to
the sovereign power of the government to create full legal-tender money in payment of
debts.

During the Civil War the greenbacks were made legal tender for all debts, public and private, except duties on imports and interest on the public debt. It was contended after the war that, although money was the creation of law and the power to create it was an attribute of sovereignty in every independent State, yet the Constitution of the United States did not confer that sovereign power upon our Government. The question was most elaborately discussed and decided by the Supreme Court of the United States in the legal-tender cases, and the doctrine of the Mixed Money case was not only approved, but it was declared that the United States could make full legal-tender money of paper or of any other material in peace or war; that the whole matter rested in the discretion of Congress, and that no law which Congress might pass creating legal-tender money could be questioned by the courts. Similar decisions have been made by nearly every civilized country in the world. The power to create legal-tender money by law, without regard to the material used, is fully settled and established by the concurrence of the highest tribunals of all civilized nations, ancient and modern.

The contention maintained by the fading intellectual capacity of economists, or by the selfish cunning of money getters, that gold is money, must be regarded in the same light as the contention that the world was flat; or that witchcraft was a well known device of the devil. The worship of gold, and the spoliation of the masses by the classes, are kindred illustrations of the afflictions through which struggling humanity is compelled to pass in establishing justice, liberty and equality.

Emphasis is placed on the all-important truth which the Supreme Court of the United States has settled by repeated decisions, namely, that it is the law of the land that whatever Congress declares to be money is such to all intents and purposes, without regard to the question as to what material is used, whether it be gold, silver, paper, parchment, or any other substance, upon which the edict of sovereignty can be manifested by the stamp of the Government. Those who teach otherwise not only exhibit their ignorance or evil design, but sow the seeds of anarchy and discord to overthrow and subvert the law of the land, which every good citizen is bound to obey. The cunning few, generally calling themselves bankers, who deny the right of the Supreme Court to declare what the law is, contend that the United States has no power to create legal-tender money. This they do in order to exercise the power of the Government to issue money for private gain at the expense of the public weal. These are the real anarchists who threaten the stability of our Government.

The power which creates money and compels all creditors to receive it in payment of debts is the same power which creates many other intangible functions of vast importance to the human race. It is the same power which creates municipal law, commanding what is right and forbidding what is wrong. The law which inflicts the penalty of death for murder is not a material thing, but a function. The same is true of the great body of the laws of any country, both civil and criminal. There is no material whatever, whether gold, silver, paper or anything else, which a creditor might not be compelled to take in discharge of an obligation due him if the law so commanded. The confusion arises because the money function has been conferred upon a great variety of commodities, such as gold, silver, copper, lead, paper, cattle, slaves, shells, fish, and the like. But the subject is made plain when we reflect that it was not the commodities which were money, but the force of law, or custom amounting to law, which these commodities were selected to represent, that did the work of money.

The function of money in interchanging commodities is an intermediate service which is a double transaction. Commodities are bought with money, which constitutes one-half of the exchange. The commodities so bought are then sold for money, and thus the exchange is complete. Before there can be a demand for property money must be demanded and procured. Consequently, there is no demand for property without a preceding demand for money, and, therefore, the demand for money is equal to the demand for all other things. Every intelligent human being is striving to get money, not for the purpose of consuming it, but for the purpose of using it to supply his various wants. Nothing can be done without money. Money is necessary to buy the comforts of life, to conduct commerce, to carry on war, to maintain government, and, in short, to do anything and everything needful to enjoy what others produce, and supply the innumerable wants of a person in organized society.

This great intermediate power which makes associated effort possible has no more analogy to commodities than the vitality which animates material forms and gives them life has to the ashes of the dead after life has departed.

VALUE.

Commercial value is the only value to be considered in economic science, and in this treatise the numerous misleading uses to which the term is applied, will be disregarded. Value, in a commercial and economic sense, is the mutual estimation of persons in making an exchange of commodities. In other words, the concurrent estimation of the parties making an exchange of commodities is the value of each commodity exchanged expressed in the other.

Great confusion exists in the public mind on account of the improper application of the word "value." It is frequently said, ignorantly or for the purpose of deception, that good money must be composed of some material having intrinsic value. Many well-disposed people, not knowing that value is extrinsic and not intrinsic, are misled by the use of the term as applied to value. If they would reflect they would readily see that value, in an economic sense, can only relate to property which is limited in quantity and for which there is a demand that cannot be supplied without sacrifice. If value were intrinsic it would hardly be contended that air does not contain more intrinsic value than gold. Should any one doubt this, let him consider which one he could dispense with with the least injury to himself.

The fact that there is a large class of persons in the United States who believe or profess to believe that value is intrinsic would be incomprehensible if the history of every age did not exhibit similar folly which subsequent ages have treated with ridicule and contempt. The people who promulgate this belief speak as fluently of the regulation of value by the law of supply and demand as do those who believe that value is extrinsic and not an inherent quality. The consideration that if value were intrinsic in gold it would be unchangeable, and that if all the mountains were gold an ounce of it would buy the same amount of wheat or any other commodity as it now does, makes no impression whatever upon such empirics as the Clevelands and Harrisons, or the Sumners of our colleges, or their followers, who maintain the absurd doctrine of intrinsic value.

The intrinsic quality of a glass of water at a mountain spring is equally as great as the intrinsic quality of a glass of water on the Colorado desert. A glass of water is free at the spring and commands nothing in exchange. But a glass of water on the desert may command an exorbitant price when the traveler is perishing with thirst and has plenty of money to buy it.

In an economic sense, it is as impossible to express value as existing in a single object as it is to express distance in a single point. In value more than one thing is necessary. There can be no estimation of the relation of objects where only one object exists, and there can be no distance without extension. The argument attempting to show that value is intrinsic and unvarying in gold, when reduced to its last analysis, is only the assertion that an ounce of pure gold is always worth an ounce of pure gold. A moment's reflection will show that every commodity measured by itself will always be equal to itself.

The function of money is not to act as a measure of itself, but to be a common denominator of all other valuable things. Why are the market reports published and universally read by the business community if such reports do not show the value of commodities expressed in money? If value were intrinsic and existed in the things bought and sold, and was not fixed by the estimation of the buyers and sellers, why publish market reports? If value is intrinsic, why not learn from an examination of the commodities themselves how much they will fetch in the market, instead of following the price of things bought and sold as shown by the daily reports?

PRICE.

Price is the relation between money and property, expressed in terms of money. The demand for money is equal to the demand for all other things offered for sale, because nothing can be bought until the purchaser has acquired the means of payment, either in cash or in obligations which are money futures. Consequently every demand for property follows a previous demand for money. All the property for sale and all the money in circulation are reciprocally the supply of and demand for each other. The paramount consideration in economic and monetary science is to maintain at all times as nearly as possible the same relation between the property for sale and the money in circulation, because if the volume of money is increased or decreased in the same proportion that property for sale is increased or decreased the general range of prices will remain substantially stationary. Prices of particular articles will rise and fall according to the demand for and supply of such articles; but when all the property for sale taken together is considered, the general level of prices is controlled by the volume of money in circulation.

John Stuart Mill, in the second volume of "Mill on Political Economy," page 2, says:

"As the whole of the goods in the market "compose the demand for money, so the whole "of the money constitutes the demand for "goods. The money and the goods are seeking "each other for the purpose of being ex- "changed. They are reciprocally supply and "demand to one another. It is indifferent "whether, in characterizing the phenomena, "we speak of the demand and the supply of "goods or the supply and the demand of "money. They are equivalent expressions."

And, again, on page 18, he says:

"That an increase of the quantity of money "raises prices and a diminution lowers them is "the most elementary proposition in the the- "ory of currency, and without it we should "have no key to any of the others."

Some writers criticise this doctrine, but nothing which they say militates against the general principle that an increase in the volume of money tends to raise prices and a decrease to lower them. They suggest, for example, that the volume of metallic money in the world was more than doubled between 1850 and 1873 by the gold from California and Australia, and that general prices rose only about twenty per cent. They do not make proper allowance for the change in conditions which is made by every increase in the volume of money. General prices fell between 1810 and 1850 about fifty per cent. by reason of the Spanish-American wars, which greatly diminished the output of the precious metals, and at the time of the new discoveries general prices were rapidly declining. The new gold not only checked the decline, but actually produced rising prices for nearly a quarter of a century. The reason why the new gold did not double general prices was because the new money enabled the people at large to buy more of the products of labor, and thereby greatly increased the market for such products. The opportunity thus afforded to sell, stimulated production enormously and increased the supply of property nearly as rapidly as the new gold added to the volume of coin. Thus, new productions fed a growing market, and nearly balanced the increase of the volume of money which the new gold produced. General prices were not inflated, but were substantially stable, with an upward tendency.

Since the mints have been closed to silver and one-half of the supply of the metallic money cut off, there has been a general decline of prices of more than fifty per cent., showing that general prices conform to the volume of money, whether it be increasing or decreasing. An increasing volume of money may so stimulate production as to prevent a rise in prices corresponding with such increase, but every diminution of the volume of money operates with full force in depressing general prices, because a shrinking volume of money reduces the aggregate amount of money available for the purchase of property and injures or destroys the market, and thereby discourages enterprise and limits production. This principle is graphically illustrated in our progress toward the gold standard, which has produced a fall in general prices in twenty years of at least fifty per cent., and caused a corresponding paralysis in the productive forces of the country. More than one-half of the productive forces of the United States are dormant on account of the stagnation caused by contraction of the money supply to reach the gold standard.

The fall in general prices is admitted, but it is sometimes denied that such fall was produced by the demonetization of silver. The recent exhaustive report of the Royal Commission of England on the Subject of Agricultural Depression was unanimous in attributing the distress in that industry to the decline in prices of agricultural products, but the Commission was not unanimous as to the cause of such decline. Some of them attributed it to improved appliances in agriculture. Sir Robert Giffen, the acknowledged leader of the gold monometallists, deprecated the suggestion that the fall of prices in the last twenty years is not mainly attributable to the demonetization of silver. He called attention to the fact that the methods of production in agricultural pursuits were improved more rapidly between 1850 and 1873 than they have been since, and that notwithstanding such rapid improvement in agricultural implements prices constantly rose from 1850 to 1873. since which time, although the improvements in agricultural implements have been less important than previously, prices have fallen fully fifty per cent., which must be attributed to the demonetization of silver. It is, he contends, a delusion to attribute the decline of general prices to improved methods of production.

It is true that many articles that were costly and regarded as luxuries a few years ago are now cheap, and rank among the necessaries of life. Skill and enterprise are constantly reducing the cost of articles in use and making them cheap, while inventive genius and enterprise are constantly creating new and costly luxuries which contribute to the comfort and gratify the taste of those who can afford to have them. The costly articles invented and put upon the market every year fully balance, by the high prices they command, the reduction in prices of other things.

Justice between debtor and creditor, and equal opportunities for all, are only attainable by a volume of money which will always be sufficient in quantity to bear a constant or stable relation between all the property for

sale and all the money in circulation. The
stability of general prices, which the proper
volume of money alone can maintain, puts in
operation the entire productive forces of the
country, furnishes labor for all willing hands,
and secures prosperity and progress. The importance of furnishing opportunities to honest
labor cannot be over-estimated, because production reproduces and consumption absorbs
the wealth of a country several times in each
decade; and if production is not checked by
contraction, the surplus over consumption will
add enormously to the general wealth of a
nation.

BIMETALLISM.

The indiscriminate use of gold and silver for coinage into standard money is the use of the two metals for the single purpose of creating money, and not for the purpose of creating a double standard of money. The money of one metal has precisely the same functions in its debt-paying and purchasing power as the money of the other. It is a mistake to suppose that the exclusive use of one metal for the time being, because the other is not equally available, creates a single standard of gold or of silver. The right to coin and use the metal which is cheapest, at the option of the debtor, is the cardinal result of bimetallism. There is no more difference in the functions of the money that different metals produce than there would be in the functions of steam, whether generated by wood or coal. In the former case it is one money; in the latter it is one steam.

Parity between the two metals has nothing to do with bimetallism, but parity between the volume of money in circulation and the property for sale is of paramount importance. As long as the supply of money and the property for sale bear the same ratio to each other, the parity which equity and justice require is preserved. The coincidence of parity between the two metals during all the ages previous to 1873, when both had unlimited coinage, has led people to suppose that parity is a condition precedent to bimetallism and not a condition subsequent, produced by equal coinage laws for both metals. The reason why bimetallism produces parity is very plain. If a certain amount of money can be coined out of a given quantity of silver, and a like amount can be coined out of a given quantity of gold, such given quantity of silver and such given quantity of gold each represents the same amount of coin, and there can be no difference whatever in their value.

If it is more convenient to obtain a dollar by the coinage of 25.8 grains of standard gold than by the coinage of 412½ grains of standard silver, gold will be used for that purpose; and if a dollar can be more readily obtained by the coinage of silver, then silver will be used for that purpose. When either of the two metals becomes dearer than the other, the entire demand falls on the cheaper metal until the increased demand raises the value of that metal equal to or in excess of the value of the other, the cheaper metal being always in demand in preference to the dearer. Their rela tive value is thereby automatically equalized.

The relative production of the two metals for the last four hundreds years illustrates the fact that under the equal coinage of both their relative quantities have nothing to do with their parity. From the discovery of America to 1803, according to Von Humboldt, there were forty-four ounces of silver produced to every ounce of gold, and at no time during that whole period would an ounce of gold buy more than 15½ ounces of silver. From 1803 to 1850 there were about thirty-five ounces of silver to one ounce of gold produced, and still an ounce of gold would buy just 15½ ounces of silver, no more, no less. From 1850 to 1873 there were only six ounces of silver to one ounce of gold produced; and yet an ounce of gold continued to buy 15½ ounces of silver. At the last named date the United States and various European countries commenced closing their mints to silver, until the right of the depositors of silver bullion to have it coined into money was denied by the entire western world.

Since 1873 the production of silver bullion has been a little less than sixteen ounces to one ounce of gold, while an ounce of gold will now buy between thirty-two and thirty-three ounces of silver. It will be observed that it was the option of the debtor to have either metal coined for his use in payment of debts which maintained the parity. It will also be observed that it was the closing of the mints which took away that option and transferred the coinage demand, which both metals had supplied, to gold alone which has created the present disparity.

The only parity which interests mankind is that parity which exists between money and commodities. The parity between silver and commodities has remained substantially stationary. Four hundred and twelve-and-a-half grains of standard silver will buy very nearly as much of all things in general to-day as $412\frac{1}{2}$ grains of standard silver or 25.8 grains of standard gold would have bought twenty-five years ago, but 25.8 grains of standard gold to-day will buy more than twice as much property in general as they would have bought a quarter of a century ago. The disparity between money and property, created by the disuse of silver, has depreciated all kinds of property, caused stagnation in business, and produced universal distress. It is the greatest calamity that has afflicted the human race for more than five hundred years. The bondholders, annuitants and others enjoying fixed incomes are being unjustly benefited by this monetary revolution at the expense of all other classes of society.

Thus it is shown that open mints for the unlimited coinage of all the gold and all the silver brought to them to be converted into money without limitation or discrimination against either, and the right of the debtor to pay his debts and taxes in the coin of either metal at his option, is bimetallism.

In preceding pages it was shown that money is the creation of law, and that every sovereign state may create full legal-tender money by the use of metal, paper, or any other suitable material upon which to stamp or print the sovereign mandate. It may be asked, if paper will answer the same purpose as the precious metals, why not use paper and avoid the cost of mining for gold and silver? The reply is, that the precious metals, so long as the mines are reasonably productive, furnish a more reliable, stable and certain method of regulating the volume of money than any rule or theory advanced for limiting or regulating such volume by legislative enactment. Gold and silver have been used as money metals since prehistoric times. When the mines were productive, ancient civilization developed; and when the mines were exhausted barbarism followed the shrinking volume of money with as much certainty as night followed day.

In the zenith of her power Rome had, according to the estimate of W. Jacob, F. R. S., and the historian Gibbon, about $1,800,000,000 of gold and silver coin in actual circulation. The mines became exhausted, and the production of the precious metals for about fourteen hundred years was very limited. The supply of gold and silver in the country which had comprised the Roman Empire was reduced during that long money famine from eig' teen hundred

millions to less than one hundred and fifty
millions, and the descendants of the warriors
and statesmen of the great and glorious civilization which was strangled by fourteen hundred years of contraction became feudal slaves
and were sold with the land.

Modern civilization had its origin in the
discoveries of gold and silver in Mexico and
South America. The supply of the two metals was continuous for about three hundred
years, and a new civilization was created. At
the beginning of the present century the Spanish-American wars created a money famine by
interrupting mining in Mexico and South
America. From 1810 to 1850 all Europe was
disturbed by anarchy and civil war, and afflicted by poverty and want. The United
States was relieved to a great extent from the
horrors of the money famine, in the first half
of the present century, by the great Missis-
sippi Valley, in which our generous Government gave a farm to every man who would
take, occupy, and improve it. Millions of
hardy pioneers from Europe sought homes in
the marvelous valley of the West, bringing
with them their money and their belongings,

and by their labor and enterprise added enormously to the prosperity of the United States,
and mitigated in this country the miseries of
the money famine which sorely afflicted the
people of the Old World.

The gold from California and Australia
marked a new era in the progress of civilization, set in motion the productive agencies of
the human race, revived commerce, stimulated
learning and science, inspired invention, and
was the means of accumulating greater wealth
in twenty-five years than in any preceding
century. The automatic rule of allowing the
volume of the circulating medium to be regulated by the supply of the two metals worked
to perfection. When there was a slight decrease in the output of gold, the discovery of
the great Comstock lode revived silver mining
throughout the world, and if the product of
both metals had been used according to the
laws of the better days of the Republic and
the universal custom for thousands of years,
there would have been no shrinkage of the volume of money, no increase in the purchasing
power of dollars, or decrease in the value of
property, and the progress and prosperity of

the wonderful period of human advancement between 1850 and 1873 would have been indefinitely continued.

The power of the Government to create money by the use of paper is undoubted, but the experiment of a proper limitation of the volume of money by human laws, without the automatic rule of regulating that volume by Nature's supply of the two metals, is yet untried. The apprehension that an undertaking by the Government to substitute legislation for the automatic rule of regulating the volume of money might result in ruinous inflation or destructive contraction, is at present an insurmountable obstacle to dispensing with the use of gold and silver. The abandonment of the automatic rule by the demonetization of silver has created a necessity for further action. If only gold is to be used, the certainty in such case of re-establishing feudal slavery in Europe and America and destroying every vestige of free institutions, ought to induce all intelligent and patriotic citizens to make a desperate effort to free themselves from the chains of financial bondage. If silver is deprived of its money functions, gold must share the same fate, and paper must be substituted for both to rescue civilization from decay.

The experiment of abandoning the precious metals for use as money is so full of doubt and danger, and the gold standard is such an ominous precursor of ruin and destruction, that an intelligent people fear to adopt either alternative. This momentous question is brought to the attention of the people by the grinding effect of continually falling prices. They compare the prosperity their ancestors enjoyed while the mints were open to both metals, and the opportunities which then existed for acquiring comfort and independence, with the bankruptcy, want, and poverty of all who are now so unfortunate as to depend upon productive enterprises for a livelihood. They are certain of relief if they reverse the legislation which caused their calamities, and re-enact the coinage laws of Jefferson and Hamilton. They must take the Constitution and the uniform custom for thousands of years for their guide if they would find the way to relief.

RATIO.

The quantity of gold compared with the quantity of silver used to make a given amount of money is called the ratio between the two metals. This ratio is purely arbitrary and depends entirely upon the discretion of the lawmakers. It is to be remembered that the aggregate weight of the silver in the world is about 15½ times as much as the aggregate weight of the gold in the world. This singular coincidence has led many to suppose that the prevailing ratios of the various nations of the civilized world are ordained by nature. Bimetallists do not base their insistence that the mints of the United States ought to be open to the coinage of gold and silver at the ratio of 16 to 1 upon any natural phenomena. They are in favor of 16 to 1 because it is the established ratio now in existence under the laws of this country, and upon the faith of which ratio the obligations of the Government are predicated. The act of July 14, 1870, under which every bond now outstanding has been issued, provides that the public debt incurred under the act shall be paid in coin of the standard value of that date. A change of ratio would be in derogation of every contract now outstanding between the Government and its creditors.

No good reason can be given for a change which would require more silver to be put in the silver dollar than it now contains. The fact that there are about $4,000,000,000 of silver coin now doing duty as money at a ratio approximating 15½ to 1 must be duly considered. If the commercial value of silver bullion, which is now denied the right of mintage, should be made the basis of a ratio, it would require all the silver coin in the world to be recoined to correspond with the new ratio, which would contract the world's money not less than two thousand millions. Such contraction would be of the same vicious character as the original demonetization of silver. It would rob the debtor for the benefit of the creditor, further paralyze enterprise, and increase the existing poverty and distress in the world.

It is constantly objected by the gold monometallists that the United States alone cannot maintain the parity between the two metals at the ratio of 16 to 1, and that, therefore, that ratio must be abandoned. The Government has nothing to do with parity other than to make equal laws. Parity between the different kinds of money in circulation does not depend upon the cost of the material of which they are made, but depends exclusively upon their relative functions. Every full legal-tender dollar will perform the same service, and is just as valuable as every other full legal-tender dollar in circulation. Nothing can make a difference in the value of full legal-tender money but a discrimination in favor of the coin of one metal and against the coin of the other. If one kind of money has useful functions which another kind of money does not possess, its value might, and almost certainly would, be greater than the money less favored by law.

The suggestion that the silver dollar would be a 50-cent dollar under free coinage at the ratio of 16 to 1 is erroneous. The United States has issued Treasury notes from time to time since 1813 and made them receivable for all public dues. Every one of such notes, which was receivable for Government dues, has at all times been at par with coin. Coin and Government notes receivable for Government dues never parted company until a provision was inserted in the legal-tender act repudiating the greenbacks to the extent of refusing to receive them for duties on imports and interest on the public debt.

There are nearly five hundred million standard silver dollars doing duty as money on a par with gold, either in actual circulation or in circulation by their representatives, silver certificates. It is stated that this is because the amount of such dollars does not exceed five hundred millions. Attention is called to what Secretary of the Treasury Sherman, the father of the gold standard, said on this subject in his report of 1879, page 14:

"The total amount of silver dollars coined to November 1, 1879, under the act of February 28, 1878, was $45,206,200, of which $13,002,842 was in circulation, and the remainder, $32,203,358, in the Treasury at that time. No effort has been spared to put this coin in circulation. Owing to its limited coinage it has been kept at par; but its free coinage would soon reduce its current value to its bullion value, and thus establish a single silver standard."

The purchase and coinage of silver bullion into standard dollars continued for about fourteen years after this declaration of Secretary Sherman, and the amount of silver coin was increased more than ten-fold without the slightest depreciation in the purchasing power of the silver dollar. This statement of Secretary Sherman is cited because it is one of the stock arguments of the advocates of the gold standard, which, like all their other contentions, is in direct opposition to existing facts.

Mr. Cleveland, after his election and before his inauguration, on February 24, 1885, addressed a letter to Hon. A. J. Warner and others, then Representatives in Congress, requesting an immediate repeal of the Bland-Allison act providing for the purchase of not less than two million nor more than four million dollars' worth of silver bullion per month to be coined into standard dollars. In that letter, among other things, he said:

"I hope that you concur with me and with the great majority of our fellow-citizens in deeming it most desirable at the present juncture to maintain and continue in use the mass of our gold coin as well as the mass of silver already coined. This is possible by a present suspension of the purchase and coinage of silver. I am not aware that by any other method it is possible."

The Bland-Allison act remained on the statute book, and the purchase and coinage of silver continued under it for more than five years before it was repealed, and the so-called Sherman act which provided for the purchase and use for the purpose of money of not less than four and a half million ounces of silver bullion each month was substituted therefor. The amount of silver coin was much more than doubled after Mr. Cleveland declared that there was no possible way of maintaining and continuing in use our gold coin except by suspending the purchase and coinage of silver. Predictions of all the leading goldites in the land to the same effect might be cited. They told the people every day while the United States was purchasing and coining silver that the limit had been reached, and that if any more silver were coined the value of the silver dollar would fall to the current price of silver bullion. The fact that they have made these false predictions for more than twenty years, and continue to make them, must be attributed to their ignorance or to their desire to deceive the public.

There is another grossly absurd dogma which goldites constantly preach and teach. This also appears in the Cleveland letter, which is said to have been the first financial document ever written for Mr. Cleveland to sign. Mr. Cleveland argued in that letter that the Bland act must be repealed, or gold would be withdrawn, the volume of money unprecedentedly contracted, and the wages of labor scaled down by their payment in depreciated money. To avoid doing him an injustice the precise language he used in predicting the results of the refusal to repeal the Bland act will be quoted. He said:

"Gold would be withdrawn to its hoarding places, and an unprecedented contraction in the actual volume of our currency would speedily take place. Saddest of all, in every workshop, mill, factory, store, and on every railroad and farm, the wages of labor, already depressed, would suffer still further depression by a scaling down of the purchasing power of every so-called dollar paid into the hands of toil."

"Unprecedented contraction in the actual volume of our currency" would hardly scale down the purchasing power of the dollar. **If contraction does not increase the purchasing power of the dollar, what does?**

The hallucination which would induce a President of the United States to believe that unprecedented contraction, creating dear money, and the robbery of the laborer by cheap money in circulation, could occur at one and the same time, accounts for many of the absurd vagaries of the advocates of so-called "sound money." But strange as it may appear, this absurd paradox has been iterated and reiterated by the so-called economists of our colleges, the financial mountebanks of the commercial press, and the controllable politicians for the last twenty years.

These examples of the false predictions of the goldites have been cited to show how little reliance can be placed upon their arguments against the unlimited coinage of silver at the ratio of 16 to 1, because the stock argument they always use, when driven to the wall by the force of well-known facts, is that the coinage ratio must be changed to correspond with the commercial ratio of the two metals. They seem entirely oblivious of the fact that under equal coinage the commercial ratio followed the coinage ratio without material variation for thousands of years previous to 1873. While the mints were open no one would sell silver bullion or gold bullion for a less amount of money than it would produce at the mint. It was impossible for either silver or gold to decline in price below the coinage value, because there was an unlimited market for it at that price. Nor could the commercial price of either of the metals rise to any appreciable extent above the coinage value, because in that case its excessive price would be prohibitory and the demand would fall on the cheaper metal until the differing commercial prices of the two metals became equalized.

The mode adopted by the goldites for the ostensible purpose of restoring the parity between the two metals is like going down a mountain to reach the summit. It was the non-use of silver which reduced the demand and created the disparity between the bullion value of the two metals. The argument that the non-use of silver and the unlimited use of gold sustains parity is a transparent fallacy and ought not to mislead the people.

The slightest reflection will show that the non-use of a commodity destroys the demand and reduces the price. Would the price of wheat be advanced if everybody should stop eating wheat bread? Yet the goldites say that the way to raise the price of silver to a parity with gold is by the utter disuse of silver and the use of gold alone.

The Harrison-Cleveland combination excused the breach of trust of which they were guilty in refusing to pay out silver according to law and the contract with the bondholders, by contending that such use of silver would destroy the parity, and that the only way to maintain the parity is to buy gold at any price and pay it to the Government creditor, and keep the silver in the vaults of the Treasury. They claim to have discovered that the unlimited use of gold and the non-use of silver will make an equal demand for both and maintain the parity. If they were indicted as private parties would be for breach of trust in surrendering the option of their employers, as the Government's option was surrendered to the bondholders, would a jury acquit them on such an absurd pretext?

MOTIVE FOR DEMONETIZATION.

The motive for the monetary revolution of 1873 was the greed of the owners of bonds and other sources of fixed incomes. The space allotted in this little volume does not permit a detailed account of the various expedients adopted to secure the demonetization of silver. It is sufficient for the present purpose to state (and it cannot be successfully contradicted), that the coinage of silver was suspended without the knowledge or consent of the American people, and without the knowledge of the people of any other civilized country. The scheme was devised and the legislation procured exclusively in the interest of those who were to be benefited by increasing the purchasing power of money and reducing the price of property. The disaster to productive enterprises and the injustice to the debtor were not considered. Blind greed kept from the view of the interested parties everything but the advantages they would gain by the measure.

An increase in the purchasing power of money in cash transactions is comparatively unimportant; but when payment is deferred, or money is borrowed to be returned at a future time, injustice will be done unless the money in circulation bears the same relation to the property for sale at the time of payment as it did at the time the obligation was created. More injustice is done by dishonest changes in the measurement of time contracts than by all other methods by which the earnings of the masses are transferred to the classes without consideration. Every other contrivance whereby the cunning of the few takes advantage of the many sinks into insignificance when compared with the wholesale spoliation which is practised through the manipulation of the volume of money in order to change the value of debts.

The manipulators who make war on the people by contraction may be likened to the invaders of the ancient empires where cultivation could only be prosecuted by irrigation. As the legions of Greece and Rome, each in turn, desolated the empires of the East by destroying the reservoirs, canals and aqueducts which watered and fertilized their fields, while pillaging and robbing the people, so they destroy the instrument of future production who reduce the volume of money to increase the obligation of contracts.

In 1873 the supply of legal-tender money in the world consisted of all the gold and silver brought to the mints for coinage, and more than $100,000,000,000 of obligations were then in existence predicated upon such supply. The demonetization of silver cut off half the supply, while the demand, by the growth of population and business, was constantly increasing. The demand is now more than double that of twenty-five years ago, as compared with the supply of coin, and consequently the purchasing power of each dollar has been enhanced more than 100 per cent. Much the larger part of the world's indebtedness existing when silver was demonetiezd is still unpaid. While some of it may have been liquidated, the aggregate has been largely increased by adding interest to principal. The national debts of the world which, twenty-five years ago, were about $22,000,000,000, now aggregate about $30,000,000,000. It cannot be denied that the national debts and all other indebtedness which existed at the time silver was demonetized were predicated upon the quantity of money furnished by gold and silver, and that the debtor had the option to pay in money of either metal.

The suggestion that a large amount of the present indebtedness of the civilized world was contracted on a gold basis is a mistake. We have not reached a gold basis, and will not until the $3,600,000,000 of full legal-tender silver shall have been deprived of its money functions and the business of the world reduced to the narrow basis of gold alone. While the approach to the single gold standard continues, the so-called gold basis will be constantly changing and always in the same direction. The conversion of Austrian silver bonds into gold bonds during Cleveland's administration greatly enhanced the purchasing power of gold by increasing the demand. The adoption of the gold standard by Japan had the same effect. It is now seriously proposed to buy gold enough to put India on a gold basis. India has about $1,000,000,000 of full legal-tender silver. The amount of gold which would be required to make the change in India alone would consume the entire output of gold available for coinage for more than a decade. The grinding process of requiring one nation after another to sell its silver coin and buy gold coin keeps the purchasing power of gold constantly increasing and the price of property constantly falling.

When we consider the world's indebtedness of every kind, public and private, now estimated at about $150,000,000,000, the tremendous loss to the debtor and gain to the creditor by the constant increase of the purchasing power of money, surpasses the wildest imagination. It is difficult to distinguish the moral culpability of tampering with the volume of money, by which time contracts are measured, from the guilt of forgery by changing the figures on bank checks. Why should the former offence be called honest while the latter is denounced as a felony?

If the dealers in gold are utterly oblivious of their own wrong-doing, or so thoroughly absorbed by avarice that the suffering of the masses are wholly immaterial to them, they will do well to reflect upon the possible retribution in store for them and their posterity. Security for property rests on justice and equality. The injustice of changing the measure of time contracts by a change in the money standard is so flagrant, so far-reaching, so destructive of the peace and happiness of the great mass of the human race that it weakens confidence, creates envy and distrust, embitters the masses against the classes, disturbs the foundations of society, and threatens the stability of governmental authority.

MONEY IS NATIONAL.

The expressions "money good all over the world," "the best money of the world," and the like, emanating from leading statesmen and financiers, are misleading. There is no money good all over the world. No money can possess money functions outside of the country of its creation, unless they are conferred upon it by the local law of the country to which it is taken. We recall but a single instance where an attempt has been made to create international money. The so-called Latin Union, consisting of France, Greece, Italy, Belgium, and Switzerland, entered into a treaty in 1865 whereby each of these governments was bound to treat the coinage of all the others as full legal-tender within its jurisdiction. It required the law of each of these governments, or a treaty having the force of local law, to make creditors receive this money outside of the country in which it was coined.

It is not unusual, however, for a government to create money out of the coins of other nations by making them legal-tender. This was done by the United States in 1793, by the act which made all the foreign gold and silver coins legal-tender in this country, according to their weight and fineness. In consequence of that act the great mass of the silver coin current in the United States previous to 1857 was foreign coin. Spanish-American countries from which we obtained our silver charged an export duty on silver bullion and made it an inducement for the owners of it to take it to their mints before exporting it to the United States; consequently, most of the silver received in the United States was in the shape of coin. The coinage of the United States was principally confined to the recoinage of worn-out or mutilated foreign coins. In February, 1857, Congress passed an act declaring that foreign coins should no longer be a legal-tender in this country. This deprived the banks of coin for the redemption of their notes, and was the principal cause of the panic of 1857.

It is seen that the foreign coins which were once current in this country obtained their money function from the laws of the United States, and not from the laws of any foreign

country. The suggestion that one country
can, by its laws, make money which will be
good, as money, in any other country, ought
not to require contradiction, and would not be
noticed if the assertion that we must have
"money good all over the world" did not imply
that our financial legislation must be in con-
formity with the legislation of other countries,
which, if desirable, would be impracticable because the laws of nations are as diverse and
conflicting on the money question as on any
other matter of municipal legislation. Neither
the gold coin nor the silver coin of the United
States is money outside of the jurisdiction of
this country.

It is a mistake to suppose that trade and
commerce are carried on between countries by
the use of money as such. Money outside of
the jurisdiction creating it is as much a commodity as wheat, pork, or beef. Gold and
silver, whether coined or uncoined, are sold in
foreign countries by weight. The value of
money, as such, all over the world is regulated
by its purchasing power in the country creating it, less the difference of exchange. If it
is stamped or printed on a material in great

demand in other countries for coinage into money, such coinage demand may affect the price of the bullion in foreign markets as a commodity. The mints of the commercial world being generally open to convert gold into coin without charge for mintage, the price of gold bullion in foreign markets is the same as its coinage value. Money made of silver or paper must be sent back to the country creating it, where it will pay debts and taxes, and, consequently, such money is always at a discount equal to the difference of exchange. It is the business of exchange to convert the money of one country into the money of another country. Every banking institution doing an exchange business will inform a customer without delay how much American money it will take to buy a thousand rubles in Russia, a thousand rupees in India, or a thousand yens in Japan, and the banks engaged in the business of exchange in those countries will as readily inform their customers how much of their money it will take to buy a thousand American dollars in the United States.

Foreign commerce consists of the exchange of commodities. Everything that goes from one country to another through the channels of commerce goes for the purpose of exchanging the commodities of one country for the commodities of another. It requires two transactions to make a foreign exchange, the same as it does to exchange commodities at home. Our goods are sent to France, for example, and sold for French money. It makes no difference whether we send gold, silver, cotton, or pork. When we have acquired French money the transaction of exchange is only half consummated. We then buy French goods with the French money which we have thus acquired. This double transaction completes the exchange of our commodities for the commodities of France. The only interest we have in French money is to know that it will buy French goods and how much, and the only interest the French people have in our money is to know that it will buy American goods and how much.

There can be no doubt that gold as a commodity is a convenient export on account of the extensive demand for it in foreign countries for coinage into money. Besides, we know in advance how much money our gold bullion will fetch in foreign markets because its price is already fixed by their mint laws. This was equally true of silver for thousands of years previous to 1873. The price of all other kinds of money must be determined by market conditions independent of local laws. The price of silver was substantially the same in all countries, while enough mints were open to the unlimited coinage of both metals to maintain the bimetallic tie and make the coin of the two metals practically one money.

The mint privileges of gold in foreign countries, which make gold bullion equivalent to coin in their markets, does not add to its desirability as a circulating medium in the countries where it is coined. When paper and silver are endowed with the money function they are more reliable and safer for use as money than gold. Take, for example, the silver coins and silver certificates of the United States. They perform all the functions of money at home which gold can perform, and we have seen that our gold coin has no money functions abroad. The habits of silver and paper money are much better than the habits of gold money. They are domestic in their nature and are found at home when required for use. They do not run away and get locked up by the financial poundmasters on the other side of the Atlantic. All the people know how faithfully silver certificates stay at home and circulate from hand to hand. No raids on the Treasury are made with them. They are the best possible money for every purpose, except manipulating the market and stock jobbing.

The dealers in gold are very much opposed to silver certificates, or any other kind of money which they cannot impound in foreign countries, and then compel the United States to issue gold bonds with which to buy it back and bring it home. When our gold goes to England it is converted into English coin without charge, and becomes English for both commercial and war purposes. The same is true when it goes to France and Germany; it becomes French or German coin as readily as it becomes English coin, through the naturalization laws of the mints of those countries. All other kinds of money except gold must necessarily have a home and a country. No kind of money but gold can be naturalized in foreign mints and made an enemy of the

United States. Our laws creating money are known and recognized all over the world, and any money current in the United States will sell in any foreign country for its value in this country, less the difference of exchange. No money except gold will desert the flag and stay abroad and fight the battles of other countries. Gold will never be the best money that can be made until there is some law to punish it for desertion.

Various countries have at different times put an export duty on their gold coin to keep it at home. Others have charged seigniorage on coining, thereby making gold coin more valuable for home use than for export. Gold is such a confirmed traitor that every civilized nation in the world has been compelled to banish it in times of great emergency. Every modern state has been compelled in time of war to use its sovereign power to create money which would stay at home and fight its battles. No great war involving the existence of a nation has ever been fought with gold or on a gold basis. Silver, while the mints were open, might be exported to the injury of the country coining it, but not to the same extent as gold could be exported. It was a very much better money than gold in time of war, on account of its bulk, its denomination, and the distribution of its coins. It could not be easily gathered up into great hoards or transported. Gold was always the money of the speculative class, who seldom fight the battles of their country. While the mints were open, silver was the money of those who created the wealth of a nation in time of peace and fought its battles in time of war.

It is almost impossible to exaggerate the injuries done to a country by the wholesale export of its money. The export from this country of about a hundred millions of gold to Austria in 1892-3, to form a reserve to enable that country, through the Rothschilds syndicate, to convert $2,400,000,000 of Austrian silver bonds into $2,800,000,000 of gold bonds, was most disastrous. The panic which it produced injured the people of the United States thousands of millions, and its baneful effects are still everywhere visible. If our Government had exercised its stipulated option to redeem its notes either in silver or gold, by refusing gold for export, no gold would have been exported, and the panic of 1893 would not have occurred. What stronger argument can be made against an exclusively gold "money good all over the world," or, which amounts to the same thing, money made of a material convenient for export and which can be converted into the money of all countries without loss, than the object lesson of the panic of 1893 caused by the export of our gold?

The contention that gold is necessary to carry on foreign commerce is one of the false and deceptive dogmas of the gold monometallists. While gold was at a premium, and the Indian mints were open to the coinage of silver, Indian commerce with foreign countries increased without a parallel. The year preceding the suspension of coinage in India that country exported sixty million bushels of wheat, fifty-three million dollars' worth of raw cotton, fifty million dollars' worth of textile fabrics, and vastly more jute and opium than ever before. She paid eighty million dollars of gold interest in London without increasing taxation. Since the suspension of silver coinage her exports have declined, her foreign debt has been greatly augmented, and millions of her people have starved to death for want of money to buy food, although there was abundance of rice to be had for a cent a pound and plenty of wheat in the market at a less price than the cost of production in this country. Chile and Japan are to-day suffering all the miseries of financial depression on account of the suspension of the coinage of silver and the adoption of the gold standard, while Mexico, with her mints open to the coinage of both metals, presents an object lesson of prosperity surpassing the success of any other country in the nineteenth century, when her condition twenty years ago is taken into consideration.

A foreign demand for the wheat, cotton and other products of the farm enhances the price of such commodities, stimulates their production, increases the demand for labor, brings money into the country, and furnishes a market for the products of the mills, factories, foundries, and all other industrial establishments; whereas a foreign demand for gold, which takes away our money, reduces the price of all our commodities, bankrupts the debtor, and produces stagnation, misery and want.

The pathetic appeal of our ex-Presidents in behalf of the laboring masses of this country for "money good all over the world" seems to assume that laboring men do their marketing in Europe. These monometallists would do themselves more credit if they would frankly tell the people that gold for export would create a scarcity of money at home and make it more difficult for them to obtain any kind of money with which to pay their bills at the grocery.

The historian of the future will be bewildered when he compares the financial teachings of Aristotle with the dogmas of the gold monometallists of our time, who contend that the commodity gold is money in and of itself, and that good money cannot be created by the use of any other material. If he should attempt to make dates correspond with the condition of civilization, he would probably assign the teachings of the gold monometallists to a period long anterior to the building of the pyramids, and the teachings of Aristotle to the age of railroads, telegraphs, telephones, and other marvelous inventions which now control the forces of nature.

PARITY.

All the commercial nations of the world conducted their commerce on the bimetallic standard previous to 1873, although some of them did not coin both metals; but the nations which did coin both metals maintained the parity between gold and silver at the ratio of about $15\frac{1}{2}$ to 1 throughout the world. In the language of the Royal Commission of England, the coins of the two metals for commercial purposes were regarded as one money. The fact that England and Portugal did not coin silver, and that India and other Asiatic countries did not coin gold, did not destroy the bimetallic tie so long as the United States and France and other European countries coined both gold and silver without limitation or discrimination against either metal. France, especially, acted as the great clearing-house of the world for gold and silver for more than seventy years previous to 1873. No one in any part of the world having either gold or silver bullion would part with it for a less amount of money than it would produce at the French mint.

After the United States and France and the other nations of Europe closed their mints against silver there was no commercial nation where both gold and silver bullion could be converted into coin for the benefit of the owner. The bimetallic tie which made gold and silver one money for commercial purposes was broken and the value of each metal was regulated by the demand for coinage in the countries which accorded it the privilege of mintage. The demand of the United States and Europe for the purpose of coinage fell on gold alone, while the demand for coinage purposes of Asia, Mexico and South America nearly all fell upon the white metal. There was a greater demand for gold in the gold-standard countries in proportion to the supply of gold than there was for silver in the silver-standard countries in proportion to the supply of silver. There was no great national clearing-house to maintain the bimetallic tie and the bullion value of the two metals was regulated by the demand for each in proportion to the supply. The inadequate supply of gold in the gold-standard countries has raised the price of that metal fully one hundred per cent.

above the level of prices for commodities, but the demand for silver in the silver-standard countries has not exceeded the supply as shown by the stability of general prices in those countries.

The rupee in India, from 1873 to 1893, when its coinage was suspended, was as stable in its value or purchasing power as any money which ever circulated. It upset the theories of the empirics of the gold-standard school because it refused to fluctuate, and the general level of prices, expressed in rupees, remained substantially stationary. They called it the "perverse rupee," because its purchasing power was substantially the same while the mints of India were open to the unlimited coinage of silver. But the rise in the purchasing power of gold in the gold-standard countries, while the purchasing power of silver remained stationary in the silver-standard countries, produced a difference of exchange. This difference of exchange has been constantly increasing as one country after another demonetized silver and joined the gold standard countries, thereby enlarging the demand for gold and decreasing the demand for silver. If a sufficient number of the commercial nations now on the gold standard would open their mints to silver and abandon gold to equalize the demand for the two metals in proportion to the supply of each, parity would be restored, but it would probably be impossible to maintain such parity without the bimetallic tie which some great commercial country would afford if its mints were open to the unlimited coinage of both metals.

Without a bimetallic nation to act as a clearing-house of exchange the relative value of the two metals would fluctuate with every increase of demand for or supply of either. France performed the function of a clearing-house between the gold-standard countries and the silver-standard countries for seventy-five years, because, as already remarked, no one would part with either silver or gold bullion for a less amount of money than could be procured at the French Mint. It is very probable that the United States, with double the population and resources of France, by adopting free coinage at the ratio of 16 to 1, could restore the bimetallic tie and maintain substantial parity between the coins of the two metals. Free coinage of silver in the United States would not only enormously increase the demand for silver and diminish the demand for gold, but it would restore the parity so long as no person would sell his silver bullion or his gold bullion for a less amount of coin than it would produce at the United States Mint. If the parity should not be restored by unlimited coinage of the two metals in the United States, the effect of independent action by this country would force enough European countries to open their mints to silver and restore the bimetallic tie to again make the coins of gold and silver one money for commercial purposes throughout the world.

FOREIGN COMMERCE.

The increase of the supply of money which would result from the unlimited coinage of silver at the established ratio would so stimulate the productions of the farms and workshops of this country as to enormously enhance the demand for the products of labor at home by furnishing money to enable the people to buy and satisfy their wants, now unsupplied. It would at the same time vastly increase our exports, because the natural resources of the United States and the skill and energy of the American people, with a proper volume of money, would enable this country to pay higher wages and advantageously undersell any other country in the world in many, if not all, of the staple products of industry. If, happily, we could obtain a sufficient supply of silver to dispense for the time being with the use of gold for speculative purposes (for we use it for no other), and increase the volume of money sufficiently to raise the level of prices above the European level, we know by the object lesson furnished by other countries that

Europe would be forced to open her mints to the coinage of silver or suffer bankruptcy, while we would be more prosperous than ever before.

Attention is again called to India, Japan, Chile and Mexico to show the marvelous advantage which silver-standard countries enjoy over those bound down to a shrinking supply of gold coin. Free coinage of silver in India enabled her to develop her industries and prosper, while gold-standard England was closing her factories because she was unable to compete in the Oriental market with the Hindoos. The advantages which silver-standard India had over gold-standard England are shown by the proceedings of the Industrial Associations of the British Isles and the debates in Parliament in favor of legislation to equalize the difference of exchange. The difference of exchange between India and England on account of the enhanced purchasing power of gold was the evil complained of by the business men and manufacturers of the home government, as shown by their petitions to Parliament. The reason for the suspension by Great Britain of the coinage of silver in India,

and for the futile attempts which are still being made to put India on a gold basis, is the
alleged necessity of removing the advantages
in trade, commerce and manufacture which
the free coinage of silver gave India over the
inhabitants of the British Isles. Chile was
the most prosperous and progressive of the
countries of South America while gold and
silver could be coined at her mints on equal
terms. In an hour of folly she demonetized
silver and has since fallen into depression and
commercial decay. Japan was aroused from
her sleep of centuries by the stimulus which
the free coinage of silver gave her after the
United States and Europe were forced into
stagnation by the single gold standard. The
difference of exchange which Japan enjoyed in
trading with foreign countries, and the impetus
which the increasing volume of money gave her
home industries, enabled her with marvelous
speed to advance to a first-class power. She,
like Chile, has fallen by the wayside and
adopted the gold standard, and her glory is
departing through the agonies of depression
and bankruptcy. Mexico, by the free coinage
of silver, has risen in twenty years from the

lowest depths of depression and poverty of industries to the enjoyment of a degree of prosperity unknown in the land of the Montezumas.

The contention that an adequate supply of money promotes internal trade and stimulates business at home has never been successfully questioned. A volume of money which will sustain the stability of general prices is just as necessary in foreign commerce as in domestic trade. An inadequate supply of money means disaster in trade and commerce, whether foreign or domestic. It means stagnation, enforced idleness and poverty. Successful production without sufficient money is an impossibility. Want of money is the primary cause of failure. The reason is that money is the instrument of production. Production is conducted through the agency of money. Money buys everything which enters into the production of commodities, including the wages of labor. Money, therefore, must precede the production of commodities both for consumption at home and for export to foreign countries. When the volume of money is sufficient to maintain stability of prices at home, production will be stimulated and the resources of the country will be developed and made available for foreign markets as well as for domestic use. An inadequate supply of money retards production and adds to its cost, while an adequate supply of money adds to production and reduces the expense. This is why the Textile Fabric Associations of England could not compete with the manufacturers of India while the Indian mints were open, and this is why Europe could not successfully compete with the United States under free coinage by independent action if gold should go to a premium. It is a common saying among the financiers of Europe that the difference of exchange betweeen gold-standard countries and silver-standard countries amounts, in effect, to a bounty on the exports of the silver-standard countries and a tax on their imports.

LABOR INTERESTS.

Gold monometallists assure the laboring men that it is to their advantage to enhance the purchasing power of money, because it will make property of every kind cheaper. It is true that the dearer money is the cheaper property will be, and that the greater the purchasing power of money the more a given amount of money will buy of the necessaries of life. There can be no doubt that people who have fixed incomes—whether derived from interest on money, from annuities, or from permanent employment at fixed salaries—are benefited by dear money and cheap property, but cheap labor must be the result of cheap property. The fact that a laborer, while he has employment, can buy more of the necessaries of life with his wages does not mean that dear money and cheap property are blessings to the laboring man. The efforts of labor organizations may for a time keep up the price of day wages, and those who can find work may enjoy a temporary benefit, but the struggle of the employer against his employes to force down the wages of labor to correspond with the general range of prices will never cease until the wages of labor and the prices of property find a common level. The laborers in the United States as a whole are not now receiving within a given length of time fifty per cent. as much in the aggregate as they would if the volume of money in circulation were sufficient to develop the resources of the country and create general prosperity. Very few wage-earners are receiving the same wages which they formerly did, and those that have employment are seldom allowed to work full time. There are millions out of employment entirely, and hundreds of thousands, if not millions, of those who find work are forced to be idle a large part of the time.

The more important consideration, however, affecting the conditions of the laboring masses is the opportunity which an adequate supply of money and stable prices afford to escape from the condition of wage-earners by successfully entering into industrial pursuits on their own account. A shrinking volume of money cuts off all opportunities for advancement among the laboring classes, because, if

the property they produce by their industry
and enterprise is constantly growing less and
less in value, profits which good prices would
afford and without which accumulations are
impossible are converted into loss. Falling
prices under the gold standard compel consoli-
dations and combinations of persons engaged
in the same pursuit. Self-preservation compels them to combine their efforts and monopo-
lize the business, which destroys individual
opportunities. Nearly every line of business
in the United States has been consolidated
into combinations or trusts under the baneful
influence of the gold standard, as a means of
self-preservation. This has cut off the opportunities which were once open to all to ac-
quire wealth and independence. The privileges which the people of this country enjoyed
to better their conditions and increase their
comforts are passing away, and the conditions
of the Old World, where the rule is: "Once a
laborer always a laborer, to the remotest gen-
eration," are becoming insurmountable obsta-
cles to advancement in this boasted land of
equal opportunities.

The condition of the wage-earner does not depend so much upon the rate of wages as upon constant employment for himself and all other wage-earners. Above all, it is of paramount importance that he shall have an opportunity of acquiring property and becoming a proprietor instead of a mere drudge.

From every point of view the equal and unlimited coinage of both metals would be beneficial. It would increase the volume of legal-tender money, stop falling prices, furnish opportunities for honest industry, and add to the comfort and happiness of the American people. Under it the United States could maintain a higher level of wages and undersell in foreign markets all the gold-standard countries in the world, because our industries would be freed from the grinding process of a shrinking volume of money. Our productions and our exports would be vastly increased, the demand for labor would furnish employment for every willing hand at higher wages, the money which would be paid for labor would be abundant to secure the comforts of life, and the laudable ambition of laboring men to rise above the hard condition of the day laborers of the Old World would be gratified.

BANK CURRENCY.

The issuance of paper money is the most lucrative business invented by the genius of man. When the Government issues a million dollars of full legal-tender money, puts it in the Treasury of the United States, and adds it to the circulation by paying it out for current expenses, it saves the tax-payers just one million dollars. When a bank issues a million of currency it puts a million of currency into its vaults and loans it out on good security for as high a rate of interest as possible. This transaction creates a million of wealth for the bank so long as it remains a bank, because if any portion of the issue should be sent back for redemption, other currency of an equal amount would be immediately issued. The only event in which the assets of the bank can be drawn upon on account of its circulating notes is a failure of the bank. When the bank fails the holders of the notes have a right to find what property they can which belongs to the bank. If they find nothing the entire issue of the bank will be a dead loss in the hands of innocent holders of the notes.

All the financial plans which the banks have pressed upon the attention of the country for the last few years have had for their object the substitution of bank money for Government money, to give the banks the privilege of issuing a thousand millions or more of currency and thus add to the wealth they have already accumulated under the national banking law. When they propose to issue gold bonds and buy up the greenbacks, Treasury notes, currency certificates and silver certificates, and sell the silver in the Treasury for what it will fetch, they do not tell the people that their object is to issue bank money to themselves on which to conduct the banking business to the full extent of the Government money retired. The difficulty about the success of such a scheme consists in devising means to conceal the real purpose of the banks. The elaborate, conflicting and ambiguous plan of the experts of the Indianapolis conference, the voluminous speeches, interviews, bills and recommendations of the Secretary of the Treasury, and the various other plans devised by the bank party are contrivances to confuse and bewilder the uninitiated, but when reduced to their last analysis two objects will appear: 1. To more thoroughly commit the United States to the single gold standard. 2. To retire Government money by the issuance of gold bonds and to put out in lieu thereof bank money. They are opposed to bimetallism because if both metals were used the volume of coin would interfere with the profits of the banks in issuing money and would deprive them of the power to expand and contract the circulating medium for the benefit of speculation. It must be remembered that when the banks issue money the people get none of it, it all goes into the banks for their own benefit; but when the Government issues paper money it goes into the Treasury and is paid out in lieu of taxes, reducing to that extent the burdens of the people. The contention that bank money is so much better than Government money that the people can afford to make almost any conceivable sacrifice to secure bank issues in preference to Government money, ought not to deceive anyone.

It must constantly be borne in mind that

money is the creation of law, and that it is stamped or printed on gold, silver, or paper, the same as municipal laws are printed on paper and bound in books. It must also be remembered that the quality of money depends upon its quantity. Too much inflates prices and injures the creditor; too little forces down prices, paralyzes industries and does injustice to the debtor; just enough is that volume which will maintain the stability of general prices, do justice between debtor and creditor, and secure equality before the law in the business transactions of the country.

The contention that bank money is better than Government money will now be examined. Government money is the mandate of law which compels creditors to receive it in payment of debts. It does not depend upon the wealth of the nation any more than does the law inflicting punishment for crime or the law giving a right of action for breach of a contract. Government money is absolutely good money as long as the Government exists and has power to enforce its municipal laws. Bank money cannot be clothed with all the functions of money, and its value depends upon the solvency of the bank issuing it. The only legal-tender function which bank money has is in the payment of debts due to the bank issuing it. People may be compelled to use bank money when the Government money is withdrawn, but the holders of bank notes must take the risk of the failure of the bank. Some banks remain solvent for a long time, but nearly all of them fail sooner or later and the note-holders suffer. There was so much distrust of bank issues under the old State bank system that a traveler rarely escaped suffering a discount on his money every time he passed a State line.

The present so-called bank issues are in fact Government issues, because, if the banks do not redeem them the Government must. They circulate all over the Union, not on the credit of the banks, but on the credit of the Government. Thus the bankers succeed in drawing the Government into the banking business; but unfortunately the Government owes all the debts while the bankers enjoy all the assets in the form of the bank circulation. The banks are under obligations to redeem their circulation in greenbacks, the same money which they tell us is not good money. In practice, however, the national banks never redeem their circulation, but send it to remote parts of the country, whence it seldom finds its way back. The Government alone redeems national bank circulation, which it is compelled to do when the bank fails.

There is another bad feature about the national banking law: The Government does not undertake to protect depositors, but, by allowing banks to be incorporated under Federal law, it greatly strengthens their credit and enables them to expand and draw interest on what they owe, to such an extent that when a stringency comes they are compelled to call in their loans and break their customers, if they do not fail themselves. The reserves which the law requires are of very little use. The banks are permitted to send, and do send, nearly all their reserves to banks in a few cities named as reserve cities to be loaned out at a profit. When the country banks call for the reserves they can seldom get them in times of trouble. In the great crash of 1893 all the leading banks of the United States where the reserves were held formed a combination and refused to pay the drafts of the country banks or the checks of their own customers. In defiance of law they actually issued over $40,000,000 of their own notes, and called them "clearing-house certificates" in which they offered to pay and refused to pay in anything else.

The evidence that these banking institutions co-operated with the Cleveland administration to bring on the panic of 1893 was once abundant and has not been fully suppressed, and their suspension of cash payments without objection from the Executive disclosed the dangerous character of the national banking system. If the Comptroller of the Currency had forced the banks in the clearing-house combination to pay their depositors or close their doors, it would have bankrupted the entire country, and the banks themselves would have been destroyed. Notwithstanding the object lesson thus furnished they try to make the people believe that the banks are safer than the Government. At the time of the collapse of 1893 there were outstanding over forty-five hundred millions of bank credits, on only five hundred millions of nominal reserves. What amount of cash the banks held of their depositors' money to meet this enormous volume of bank credit the country will never know. In other words, how much of the four thousand millions which remained after deducting the legal reserves was purely fictitious, and how much was secured by actual cash, must forever remain a mystery. The habit of loaning depositors' money over and over again as it is re-deposited in the bank enormously swells bank indebtedness upon which the bank draws interest. When the crash came the banks, as usual, drew in their loans and ruined their customers. Many of the banks were unable to save themselves and went down with their customers in one common ruin.

But because banks are the storm center of panics, and when unrestrained by law are the most dangerous institutions ever organized, they cannot be abolished, as they are a great convenience. They are, in fact, absolutely necessary under our modern methods of doing business. They ought not, however, to be allowed to usurp the functions of Government by the issue of money, nor ought they to be allowed to loan more of their depositors' money than can be done with absolutely safe-ty. The great trouble is that there are too many banks. This makes it necessary for them, in order to make money, to lend their depositors' money over and over again, so as to swell their indebtedness upon which to draw interest.

The remedy for scarcity of money suggested by President McKinley in his message was the creation of more banks on smaller capital. This might, and undoubtedly would, create more bank credit, but it would hasten the coming panic of ruin, bankruptcy and liquidation. If there were fewer banks, with larger reserves, the community would be just as well accommo-dated, the depositors better protected, and the calamities of panic less frequent. The banks are entitled to reasonable compensation for the convenience they furnish the business com-munity, but that compensation ought to be con-sistent with safety and fair dealing. The swelling of bank credits to draw interest on what they owe is a great temptation to banks, and it ought to be restrained within reason-able limits by law rigidly enforced. Such restrictions on the methods of doing business as would make the banks safe institutions would remove the temptation for the establishment of purely speculative banks and banks on insufficient capital, and would enable the really sound institutions to furnish the people all the accommodations required, and at the same time retain in their vaults fifty per cent. of the money of the depositors.

The organization of banks on conservative and safe principles, with strict Governmental supervision, and the exclusive issuance by the Government of the circulating medium, whether it be gold or silver or paper, required to maintain the stability of prices, would prevent panics and secure prosperity and tranquility.

∞